DISCARD

DATE DUE

FEB 2 3 2009			
NOV 2 9 2010			

FOLLETT

The
SUPER
BOWL

BLACK MOUNTAIN MIDDLE SCHOOL
9353 Oviedo Street
San Diego, CA 92129-2198

Published by Creative Education, Inc.
123 South Broad Street, Mankato, MN 56001

Designed by Rita Marshall with the help of Thomas Lawton
Cover illustration by Rob Day, Lance Hidy Associates

Photography by Allsport, Campion Photography,
Duomo, FPG International, Photri, Spectra-Action, and
Sportschrome

Printed in the United States

Library of Congress Cataloging-in-Publication Data

Stevenson, Amy
    The Super Bowl/by Amy Stevenson.
    p.   cm.—(Great moments in sports)
    Summary: Discusses the history of the Super Bowl, the formation of
the AFL and its eventual merger with the NFL, and the major events
of each game.
    ISBN 0-88682-315-3
    1. Super Bowl Game (Football)—History—Juvenile literature.
[1. Super Bowl Game (Football)—History.   2. Football—
History.]   I. Creative Education, Inc. (Mankato, Minn.)
II. Title.   III. Series.
GV956.2.S8G66   1989   89-36707
796.332'648—dc20   CIP
                                                          AC

The SUPERBOWL

AMY STEVENSON

CREATIVE EDUCATION INC.

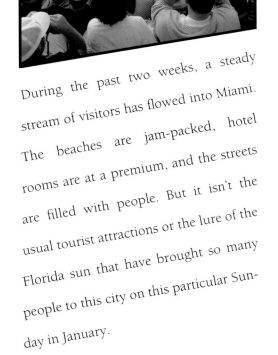

During the past two weeks, a steady stream of visitors has flowed into Miami. The beaches are jam-packed, hotel rooms are at a premium, and the streets are filled with people. But it isn't the usual tourist attractions or the lure of the Florida sun that have brought so many people to this city on this particular Sunday in January.

Today, January 22, 1989, is Super Sunday, the day that the National Football League championship will be decided in the climactic game of the season, the Super Bowl.

While the players and coaches made final preparations, spectators from around the world filled the Orange Bowl hours before game time. Meanwhile, millions of fans held Super Bowl parties at home and gathered around the television to watch the event.

Twenty-eight teams had battled all season long for the privilege of playing for the league title. The survivors were the veteran San Francisco 49ers and the surprising Cincinnati Bengals. From the opening kickoff, the game had been a close, hard-fought contest. The teams had exchanged leads several times, but now with just three minutes and ten seconds remaining in the game, the Bengals

Ickey Woods (30) drives up the middle for the Bengals.

held a three-point lead. Although the 49ers had the ball, they were buried at their own eight-yard line.

The Bengals and their fans felt that victory was close at hand. One of the Cincinnati players couldn't contain his glee. "We got 'em now," he blurted. His teammate, receiver Chris Collinsworth, knew the ending was still in doubt. He replied, "Have you taken a look at who's quarterbacking the San Francisco 49ers?"

The leader of the 49ers was Joe Montana, the quarterback who had already won two most valuable player awards in two previous Super Bowl victories. As Montana gathered the offense together in the huddle, he paused to consider his team's position. San Francisco would have to drive the ball downfield at least sixty yards to set up a possible game-tying field goal. For a victory, the 49ers would have to cover ninety-two yards and score a touchdown. With so little time remaining, neither possibility appeared likely.

The Bengals offense was led by quarterback Boomer Esiason.

Yet the odds failed to intimidate Montana. The NFL championship was at stake, and as long as there was time on the clock, he would not let his team give up. Calling two plays at once to save precious seconds, he looked at his teammates and gave them one piece of advice: "Let's get tough."

Quarterback Joe Montana

The teams lined up in formation. Montana barked out the signals and took the snap from center. As he dropped back to pass, the Bengal defense surged forward. Both teams knew that the Super Bowl championship would be determined in this drive. All the excitement and drama of the Super Bowl was captured in this one great moment.

SUPER BOWL I

The battle between the 49ers and the Bengals in Super Bowl XXIII is just one example of the many thrilling experiences that the Super Bowl has given football fans over the years. Actually, the Super Bowl is America's youngest major sports championship, yet it is without question the most popular single sports event in the nation.

The Super Bowl began its history of great moments in the very first contest, which was held in 1967. Super Bowl I featured the Green Bay Packers, the NFL's perennial champions, and the Kansas City Chiefs. The Chiefs were the best team in the American Football League, an upstart league that had challenged the NFL for both players and fans since the early 1960s. The leagues had agreed to an uneasy alliance in 1966, but pride was very much a factor as the teams prepared for this first-ever Super Bowl.

The Packers, led by their legendary coach, Vince Lombardi, were justifiably proud of their team and their league's storied history. The last thing they wanted was to lose to a team they felt was inferior to their own. On the other hand, the Chiefs saw this game as the perfect opportunity to show the world that the AFL was also a first-rate league.

As game day approached, the excitement over this historic meeting grew. "Twenty years from now I can say I was there," said Bert Coan of the Chiefs. "Just eighty boys can ever say that."

Green Bay Packers coach Vince Lombardi.

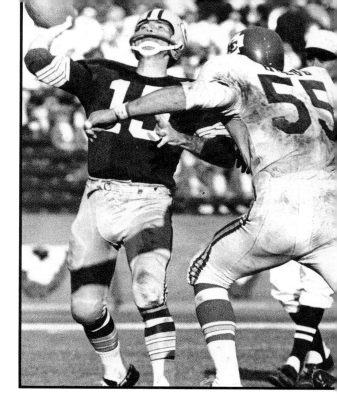

Finally, the day of the big game arrived. More than sixty-one thousand fans poured into Los Angeles Memorial Coliseum to witness history in the making.

The Packers won the coin toss and took possession of the ball. Green Bay's talented quarterback, Bart Starr, was a master at reading defenses. But this surprising Kansas City team sacked Starr for a loss twice during their opening drive. It appeared that the game would be much closer than anyone expected.

On their next offensive series, Green Bay drove down into the Chiefs' territory. It looked as though the Packers were certain to score on this drive until the team's best pass receiver, Boyd Dowler, injured his shoulder. As Dowler left the field, Lombardi turned to the bench and shouted, "McGee, get in there." Dowler's backup, Max McGee, looked up in astonishment. He had been relaxing on the bench, not paying a lot of attention to the game.

Quarterback Bart Starr was sacked twice in the opening minutes of the game.

Not expecting to see any action that day, and determined to enjoy his visit to Los Angeles, McGee had broken Lombardi's strict curfew the night before. When the coach yelled at him, he was certain Lombardi had just found out about his violation. "He's gonna chew me out right here, in front of the whole stadium," McGee recalled thinking. Instead, he was now in the game. The veteran had only made four receptions all year and was expected to retire at the end of the season. He never anticipated that he would end his career by playing a major role in the Super Bowl.

Max McGee (85) carries the football and a Chief on this run.

Play resumed after McGee joined his team on the field. Green Bay continued their march and found themselves at the Chiefs' thirty-seven-yard line. After calling the signals, Bart Starr took the snap and dropped back to pass. He threw it to his only open receiver—Max McGee. The ball struck McGee's hand and bounced upward. With Kansas City's cornerback Willie Mitchell closing in on

him, McGee caught the ball with one hand behind his back. He turned toward the end zone and lumbered thirty-seven yards for a Packer touchdown. It was the first of many great moments in the history of the Super Bowl. McGee would go on to score two more touchdowns for the Packers that afternoon as Green Bay cruised to an easy win. But his later heroics wouldn't come close to generating the excitement that his first touchdown had given the Green Bay fans.

THE GUARANTEE

Over the years, there have been many Super Bowls in which one team has come into the game as the clear favorite. These teams have often dominated play, as Green Bay demonstrated in Super Bowl I. Yet there have also been games that even the most knowledgeable football experts couldn't predict. Games that have provided some of the most thrilling and dramatic moments in Super Bowl history. Games such as Super Bowl III.

Predictions of Super Bowl winners are often turned upside-down.

This 1969 championship game matched the powerful Baltimore Colts of the NFL versus the AFL's New York Jets. By all accounts, the Colts were the superior team. The NFL team had won both Super Bowl I and II by comfortable margins. There seemed to be little doubt that the Colts would win this game as well. In fact, Baltimore was picked to win by more than twenty-one points.

The Jets, however, were led by a brash young quarterback named Joe Willie Namath. Because of his outstanding talent and personal charisma, Namath was one of the most popular figures in football. Although Namath was only twenty-five, he had already gone through a series of knee operations, which hampered his ability to move around in the pocket. Yet Namath passed with lightning quickness and pinpoint accuracy. There was no doubt he was one of the premier quarterbacks of his time.

Joe Namath hands off the ball

Despite Joe's achievements on the field, he received most of his notoriety for his colorful life-style. Nicknamed "Broadway Joe," Namath relished the New York City nightlife. In the off-season, he spent his time making movies in Hollywood instead of preparing for the next season.

"Broadway Joe" Namath

Matt Snell (41) was the Jets best runner during Super Bowl III.

As much as he enjoyed his celebrity status, Namath was serious about the game of football. He knew the Jets were a solid ball club. It upset him that few people thought his team would be able to compete with the Colts in the Super Bowl, let alone have a chance for victory. Namath was full of confidence and

wanted the world to know it. Three days before the Super Bowl, Joe made a public statement: "The Jets will win Sunday; I guarantee it."

The Colts and football fans everywhere laughed at Namath's prediction. As always, Joe had a quick comeback. "They say the Colts are going to take my statement and put it up on their bulletin board," he chuckled. "Well, if the Colts need anything to lift them up for the game, then they're in trouble." Even if the Jets were prepared, Namath had a definite game plan in mind. "We're going to get the ball and try to get a touchdown right fast. Got to get those points up on the board real quick. Yes sir, everything is going to be okay."

When Super Bowl Sunday finally arrived, the Jets showed right away that they weren't afraid of the Colts. Led by Namath's crisp passes and Matt Snell's bruising running, the Jets marched to a 7-0 lead in the second quarter. It was the first time an AFL team had ever led in a Super Bowl.

As the game progressed, Namath picked the famed Baltimore defense apart with his sharp passes and brilliant play calling. The Colts found themselves

The New York Jets offensive line dominated play against the Colts.

unable to combat the Jets and began to fall apart. Not even their legendary quarterback, Johnny Unitas, could rally the team.

"We began to panic," admitted one Baltimore player. "That's what they were supposed to do, but they didn't." Instead, the confidence Namath showed in his team gave the Jets the poise they needed to triumph over Baltimore. "Joe kept telling us we could win," said teammate Dave Herman, "and finally we believed him. Joe won it for us."

When the game ended, the Jets had prevailed by a score of 16-7. It was the first time an AFL club had ever defeated an NFL team in the Super Bowl. The New York Jets had staged one of the most unlikely upsets in professional football. It was one of the greatest moments in the history of the Super Bowl.

While some teams, like the New York Jets, have risen once to greatness to capture the Super Bowl championship, only a few teams have won the NFL title more than once. Just five teams have been the league's top team twice. And only two teams—the Pittsburgh Steelers and the San Francisco 49ers—have won the Super Bowl three or more times. The 49ers won their championships over a nine-year span with personnel that changed over time. However, the Steelers, with an amazingly talented squad, built an NFL dynasty during the 1970s, appearing in four Super Bowls. One of their greatest moments came in Super Bowl XIV.

Steeler coach Chuck Noll had put together a powerful squad. The quarterback was Terry Bradshaw, who was so strong he could throw the ball more than seventy yards. Bradshaw's talents were complemented by two strong running backs, Franco Harris and Rocky Bleier. He also had a couple of superb receivers in Lynn Swann and John Stallworth.

Terry Bradshaw is a Super Bowl legend.

Facing the "Steel Curtain."

The Steelers' defensive unit was just as impressive. Nicknamed "the Steel Curtain" because it was almost impossible for opponents to penetrate, the defense was anchored by defensive tackle "Mean Joe" Greene. There were other All-Pros on the squad as well, including linebackers Jack Ham and Jack Lambert, and defensive back Mel Blount.

Pages 20–21
Denver Broncos quarterback John Elway scrambles to make a play during Super Bowl XXII.

Their opponent in the 1980 Super Bowl was the Los Angeles Rams, who also boasted a tough defense. They were led by end Jack Youngblood and line-backer Jack ("Hacksaw") Reynolds, both known for their bone-crushing tackles. The Rams' offensive was powered by young quarterback Vince Ferragamo. Although he was untested, Ferragamo often displayed flashes of brilliance.

The Steelers came into the game as the favorites to win their fourth Super Bowl, but the underdog Rams were determined to stage an upset.

The game was nip and tuck the whole way. With little more than twelve minutes remaining in the game, the Rams held a slim 19-17 lead. Pittsburgh had possession but found themselves in a tight spot: third down and eight with the ball on their own twenty-seven-yard line.

Together, the offense and defense created a formidable team. A very successful team. They had won the Super Bowl in 1975, 1976, and 1978. "There was a point," said Greene, "where we could just look at each other and everybody knew we weren't going to lose. There wasn't a chance." "We despised losing!" Bradshaw commented. "We could not and would not accept a loss!"

Vince Ferragamo (15) looks for a receiver.

Page 23   Terry Bradshaw could throw a football over seventy yards.

The crowd stirred in their seats. It was

clear to everyone watching the contest

that this would be a pivotal play.

All-pro linebacker Jack Lambert.

Coach Noll sent in the play, "sixty prevent, slot, hook and go." Bradshaw didn't like the call because "it hadn't worked all week in practice." But it was the coach's decision. Wide receiver John Stallworth ran fifteen yards downfield, button-hooked, and went deep, getting inside cornerback Rod Perry and behind strong safety Dave Elmendorf. Bradshaw threw the ball from forty yards away, and Stallworth made an unbelievable over-the-shoulder catch in full stride. He loped into the end zone on the seventy-three-yard play.

Touchdown!

The Steelers had taken the lead. "It was crushing to play good defense and have something like that happen," said the Rams' Fred Dryer. "That can break your back." Indeed, the Steelers took command of the game and never relinquished their lead. Pittsburgh had won their fourth Super Bowl and had given their fans another special moment to remember.

John Stallworth caught the crucial pass and ran to the end zone.

THE CHAMPION

While the Steelers had proved that superior teamwork can build championship clubs, some other Super Bowls have been determined largely by a single player's contribution. Doug Williams's remarkable performance in Super Bowl XXIII is a shining example of how one player can alter the course of a championship game.

Doug Williams drops back to pass.

Williams was the quarterback for the Washington Redskins when they faced the Denver Broncos in the 1988 Super Bowl. Before joining the Redskins, however, Williams had seen his career take a number of unexpected twists.

Originally drafted by the Tampa Bay Buccaneers, Williams quickly made his mark on the expansion team. In no time at all, he proceeded to turn the team around, taking the previously hapless Bucs to three consecutive play-off berths. Due to a contract dispute, he jumped to the United States Football League following the 1982 season, staying in the league until it folded. Williams was out of football entirely in 1986. At age thirty-two, his career was seemingly over, until Redskins coach Joe Gibbs called and offered him a position as Washington's backup quarterback. Once again, Williams was starting over.

In the Super Bowl, Washington was facing the Denver Broncos. They were led by one of the NFL's best quarterbacks, John Elway. The Broncos, making their second consecutive Super Bowl appearance, were anxious to avenge the previous January's loss to the Giants.

Denver took control of the game early, scoring a touchdown within the first two minutes of play. The Redskins tried to retaliate but soon found themselves without their leader. Williams had twisted his knee. As he hobbled toward the sidelines, his dream of winning the Super Bowl seemed to disappear. By the end of the first quarter, Denver had added a field goal while holding the Redskins scoreless. It looked as though the Broncos were taking command of the game.

John Elway led the Denver Broncos to the Super Bowl in 1987, 1988 and 1990.

Through it all, he persevered. During his first season with the Redskins, he played only a single down. But in 1987, his strong arm and even stronger will to win earned him a chance to battle for the starting position. By the end of the season, Williams was the number one quarterback and had successfully guided the Redskins to the NFC championship.

Williams became the Redskins #1 quarterback in 1987.

Suddenly, the momentum shifted. As the second period began, Doug Williams limped back onto the playing field and ignited the Redskins' offense. On the very first play from scrimmage, Williams

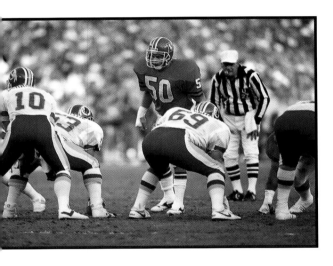

passed to Ricky Sanders for an eighty-yard touchdown. The Redskins and their fans sensed that one of the most thrilling moments in Super Bowl history was about to unfold. "You could feel the sidelines come alive," said coach Gibbs later.

After the first quarter of the game, it looked like the Broncos would win.

That play was just the beginning. Williams, in the greatest performance ever by a Super Bowl quarterback, passed for four more touchdowns before halftime. The Redskins had scored thirty-five unanswered points in less than fourteen minutes of play! The Broncos were shattered. "After the third one," said Denver linebacker Jim Ryan, "your head is spinning and it's like you're in a whirlpool." In the second half, Washington added one more touchdown to bring the final score to 42-10. The Redskins had become world champions, thanks to the fine play and inspirational leadership of Doug Williams.

A year later, Joe Montana and the San Francisco 49ers found themselves in a fight for survival. With just over three minutes remaining in the game, the 49ers had the ball at their own eight-yard line. Unless San Francisco could tie the game with a field goal, or somehow manage to score a touchdown, Cincinnati would win the Super Bowl.

Joe Montana has become the most successful Super Bowl quarterback.

Montana knew that his offense would have to execute each play perfectly to even get within field-goal range. A single mistake could prove fatal. As Montana took the snap and dropped back to pass, he focused his total concentration on the task at hand. He scanned the field and completed a seven-yard pass to Jerry Rice. The 49ers were on the move. What happened in the next nine plays and two-plus minutes was pure magic. In one of the most thrilling drives in Super Bowl history, Montana marched the 49ers eighty-two yards downfield, efficiently shredding the Bengal defense.

With just thirty-four seconds left in the game, the 49ers stood at the ten-yard line of the Bengals. Everyone in the stadium was on their feet, yelling encouragement to their team. As Montana began shouting out the signals, the Bengal defense dug in for this climactic play. The seconds began ticking off the clock as Montana dropped back and coolly fired a perfect spiral into the arms of John Taylor. The entire stadium exploded with emotion as the 49ers celebrated the touchdown. Victory was theirs! It was another great moment in Super Bowl history.

John Taylor caught the winning pass.